The Absence of Strangers

Richard Taylor

Goose River Press
Waldoboro, Maine

Copyright © 2017 Richard Taylor

All rights reserved. No part of this book may be reproduced in any form without written permission from the publisher, except by a reviewer who may quote brief passages in a review to be printed in a newspaper or magazine.

Library of Congress Card Number: 2016962987

ISBN: 978-1-59713-173-5

First Printing, 2017

Cover photo by Sally Taylor.

Published by
Goose River Press
3400 Friendship Road
Waldoboro ME 04572
e-mail: gooseriverpress@roadrunner.com
www.gooseriverpress.com

Poems here previously published

Ice River 1987
　　"Shards"

The Spoon River Poetry Review
　　"From Jane" 2007
　　"Harley in Love" 2010
　　"Harley Rides to the Altar" 2010

The Café Review
　　"Cui Dono?" 2010
　　"Carnal Knowledge" 2010
　　"Cold Knowing" 2013
　　"Coming to Mr. Kirk" 2013

Omphalos 14   2011
　　"Solitude"
　　"Thin Air"
　　"Cassander's News"
　　"A Thrush's Song"
　　"Visiting at the Mirror"

for Sally and for Jess

Table of Contents

Cui Dono?

I. The Grammar of Absence

Looking for Conversation
Sister//2
Cold Knowing//3
Visiting in the Mirror//5
April//7
Mowing//8
Haying//9
Waiting for Seamus//10
Night of Last Flowers//11
Flicker//13
The Bat//14
Cassander's News//15
Preliminary Sketches//16
Writer's Block//18
Garden Dancing//19
Curtain Call//22
Coming to Going//24
A Thrush's Song//26
January Thaw//27
Meeting House//28
Mining//29

Table of Contents

II. Signs of Affection

Harley in Love//35
Love Song of a Resected Motorcyclist//36
Harley Rides to the Altar//37
The Longing of Stones//39
Thin Air//40
As Pyramus to Thisbe//41
Adam's Lament//42
Eve Replying//43
From Jane//46
Tarzan Replying//48
Dressing for Spring's Wedding//51
Clericus at Dusk//52
The Shade Nearby//54
Poetry is the Wolf//55
Solitude//56
Parsing Her Silence//57
Tide Walker//58
Carnal Knowledge//59
Mario's First Son//60
Of Love and Baked Apples//62
Travelogue//63
A Lesson in Love at the County Fair//65
Waltzing in a Parking Lot//66
Shards//67
Rain on the Mountain//71
Looking for Dorothy//72
Forgiving//74
Tea Ceremony//75
A Diary of Sighs//76
The Musical Evening of Sister Elizabeth//77
Immaculate Conception//79

Table of Contents

III. The Fellowship of Strangers

The Choir Director Has a Talk With God//83
Winter Talk//85
Twilight of Barns//86
Veterans' Day//88
Bailey's Small Engine Repair//90
A Finnish Ice Lantern//92
Toshi's Reluctant Mushrooms//93
Walking Dawn//94
Coming to Mr. Kirk//97
Re-cycling With Clayton//98
The Agony of the Fundamentalist Apple Grower//101

Epilogue: The Absence of Strangers

Cui Dono?

after Catullus

To whom am I to give these poems,
polished, erased, smoothed again
and fitted into murmured line,
the limb and sinew
of my affection?

To you who starts my feet
galloping to the turn, racing
the dust to words, or cools
the lathered muscle, a single rein
loose in your hand—

to you who lives on the other side
of the fence, in the backyard
where the others known as you
forever tend their ground,

whose errant strand of hair
reveals unheard of wisdom
to the reticent breeze,

whose single syllable will
anchor a filament of thought, fragile
and sufficient to spin fantasies
of lace arrayed with dew,
and wait—

for whom for now I'll simply
wrap and tie a poem
around a small stone and toss it
over the hedge into
your garden full
of blossoms

and ask only that you
unfold it among your flowers
and throw the stone
back over the fence.

I.

The Grammar of Absence

Looking for Conversation

It could have been Daphne fled to the laurel tree
and I a fleet thief chasing a jeweled word,
for all that was said.

The length of a late September's amber afternoon
I listened to her heartbeat drum beneath
the satin-smooth bark

and pled the case for precious phantasy
to the garrulous leaves, until the breeze came by
with its diffident kiss.

So I went to the old maple tree
that's stood its hundred years on a green
tongue to the sea.

Its bare branches tangle with clouds and ever pray
for the clatter and rip of lightning's eye, though
its leaves are now few.

I can hush with it and listen to a bird's nest
bursting with unpracticed song, the sudden
absence of wings,

love the orange fungus it wears like a flower
where a limb once was, the room it makes for the grub
gnawing inside,

and in its crooked shade study the alphabets
of slant winds, the waves' slow wound, roots
feeding on stone.

Sister

Dinner talk is over. You go to your porch
to fill on fresh quiet by the water's edge and listen
to what the waves might have to say.

The fool wind, out again at night, boisterous
and aphasic, bothers the water's tongue to stir up
memory's bottom, its mouth full of stones.

One young wave after the other stumbles to the front,
eager to speak but just as soon shy
of its own story, goes busy erasing

the piper's footprint, smoothing sand, rolling
pebbles, striped and colored, cut
with footprints in particular mud, trilobite's skitter

to a late sun's splinters skipping from water
to water, taken away in chains of mist
into the cage of night. Tales run loose

in the surf, and no speaker arrives,
though you may imagine one talking
of tenderness and calm,

yourself perhaps,
coming into earshot.

Cold Knowing

Water from the well in a corner of our barn and house
can straighten a person up pink and suddenly
with cold astringent lacings up the eyelets of a spine.

First myself then he, we pitch the chill baptismal bucket
that binds a father to a son, blind to any firmament except
our private ivory galaxy with its few dark stars.

The soap rubs up to infant clouds around his ears,
his armpits, lathers his substantial manliness, while I
shiver in my smile, having none such to compare.

I am the altar boy to fetch the cup from the water's table
at the bottom of the dark where I see myself at a rope's length
looking back and fear to dip less than from the coldest knowing.

The bucket dropping from both hands, mouth down,
fills full, and the windlass likes its reeling up the water
clean and terrible for father in the tatters of his suds.

At a stroke redemption pure and puritanical pours
ice along his spine, sucks in his breath as every pore
slams shut, screams to a deity with no charity or name

for the cut it spends on tender flesh. I had thought
our local recompense distilled below of old
and ever since came up more mercifully parceled

in its bucket sized to a naked boy who ministers
what yet abounds of innocence, until I stand
on the other side and father comes toward me with his pail,

overfull and licking. Half my mother watches
from the window curtain, and she smiles as if uncertain
how her one becoming old will teach her other

not yet finished being young until we leap
and laugh past all proportion and exactly as a bucket
of cold knowing from the well makes naked men.

Visiting at the Mirror

How much better the newel post looks, stripped of generations
of varnish. The grain warms again, center-cut, the heart
of the cherry tree. It takes your hand, as on a child's fine hair,

with the affection you feel before ascending the stairs.
They take you to a full-length mirror on a door up there
that sees your smile coming, and lets you know more

if you pause, step in to admire, which I do, and grandfather,
the Reverend, looks back out at me. His eyes are mine,
just sunk some, my hair but thinner, crows' feet and creases

added to cheek and chin, bonier because he's been
where I'm going, taking along his big pointed ears
to prove I belong to the family tree. We both know

we're looking at the genuine article, poor as we are at hiding
what we're made of, old wood, more or less straight,
and not much fancy carving. It doesn't lie and neither does he,

being a preacher, and he remembers me in abundance
ever since I asked him what he said his last name was
when he farted in the barn. Right then he knew he'd get to do

some extra forgiving, and we both heard it in his startled
Methodist chuckle. Now he's here with the angled family
bones, parceling my present in the mirror's silvery light,

not fooled by a camera's charity and bored with its rules.
Like me, he likes to come and go across the years,
never at ease beneath the sepia stillness of a photograph.

"Just varnish to keep our secrets," he says. With that
I feel a little forgiven for acting my age and still looking
for the rest of the story, which is all you're asking for

if you're alone with a mirror and an old man and truth
that's in no hurry. Maybe that's why Grandfather came
to the mirror's door, to suggest I look over my shoulder

now and then instead of always so straight ahead. I nod,
and affection hints at reverence overdue, so I tell him
the only first hand story I have so far, how on a fine day

a woodchuck strayed into the barn, then fled from his corner
as I banged two pans. Racing the far wall to another corner,
he saw an unknown twin coming at him full tilt out of a dusty

mirror left standing there. Terror turned him sharp right, panic
pointed him at the open door, leaving his twin in the mirror
and a total stranger racing behind, banging his pans.

April

The season shifts and fear
grabs a crocus by the root, asleep
all winter and cuddling beneath the straw.

Nothing so frightening
as waking straight up
into April, pale and chilly
as a baby-sitting aunt.

All you can do is
jump out in your shocking purple
and with your orange pistils
ambush the sun.

Mowing

It is the scythe that mows the grass
when the grass inclines to lie down,
not I, for I am just a suitor
to the blade, the squeaking snath.

It is the grass that greets the blade,
summons the supple breeze,
and trunk and limb go lithe
to answer its sweet lisp.

It is the scythe that sharpens
my beginnings with the ground,
and bids the dance swing left
and back, the shuffling advance

of work boots moving up
and down the line until the grass
spreads over the August earth and spells
the swaying done to meadow's end.

The hay will hear the hone
no more. The snath
rides quiet in the crook of my arm,
the blade going home.

Haying

Before the bale took the curve of the hay away,
the lithe fork smoothed in a father's hands,
the wind's shy tune in the tines,
I caught the rising bundles as up they came,

placed them at the corners first
and then the edges overlapping in between,
and then the center where I turned about,
cross-pillowing the stack.

How I loved that haying, hot sun
on a naked back, forkfuls arcing up
like yellow paint on a giant brush
stroking the cottony clouds.

The tractor lurched, I'd tumble
into the pile and could hardly wait
for the next stop, wondering
how high I could build a load.

Then the bale arrived, too big for a boy to catch
and set just so, though surely with the lifting
I'd grow strong, my foot fall dent the tender earth,
and dance no more with the clouds.

Waiting for Seamus

The waiters drifting by in black fold up
the crumbs of conversation in their linen, stealing
cups and saucers, silverware and glasses

to the velvet shadows hurrying off
with the last of chews and sips, and we sit mute
upon the poet's word. He seems to scan

the spectral dark arriving late on slipper feet
and filling any likely ear. Perhaps he hears
a dactyl in the timid feet that scurry

hungry through a country dark. Perhaps
his candle finds some finer crumbs
hiding in a wooded Irish night,

and he has heard a rhyme. The shadows stop to listen;
not a tea cup clinks.

Dublin, 2002

Night of Last Flowers
for Sally

Night wakes the sleeping.
It is October, and the full moon calls
first frost. But a nymph
in lace nightgown knows
it is the night of last flowers.

Descending
from upstairs, she dreams
through door to porch and leaves
her bathrobe hanging on a peg to keep
her shadow warm.
                        Floating
familiar garden paths, chill crystals
catching in her hair, she visits
with nicotiana looking down and
filling the night
with fragrance, asters
deepening their purple in
the budding cold, delphiniums
their blue.
                  By blood red
cosmos all awry and echinacea
loved all day by butterflies the low
and yellow trollius has lit
the tangling shadow of sweet
honeysuckle. Steps beyond
a ruffled hollyhock in antique white
nods dowager and prim.
                          Slipperless

she glides through
silver mist to pick
with silken fingers one
or two of each,
                        and then returns
to earth and porch and slippers
with ambrosia from her other world,
puts on her shadow and her bathrobe,
tucks last gathered flowers gently
into ample parlor vase, and once again ascends
to bed.

Flicker

He drums on a poplar
forty feet up. A dreamy note not far inside
has turned his hunger for the grub to carving out
a hole that holds him, head, wings,
tail and all. Chips float down the breeze
like words crossed out, arguments defeated
in the rocking of a tree, incomprehensible
and kind.

Looking out his narrow door, the sky lies
limitless and round, and there a feathered mind
slips memory unseen from small to large
and home again on winded doubt
to brood upon a flight or phrase
turned on a porcelain sky, in a tree's
embrace, each a cup
of various hands.

The chips are fallen
to their silences, but he loves the lift
living in such vacancy, emptiness
consummated in a fresh hole wing-brushed
on the trackless air, his flash of color
on an otherwise
blank page.

The Bat

Midway through the trio's second movement,
the famous galloping rhapsody, when cello
swells to a pitch with violin and
piano runs headlong and catching up, the bat
descends from his belfry
allegro con brio!

The aerial conductor finds the players'
eyes with Brahms' own sweeping hands,
bidding the notes rise up, retreat,
come forth with him to audience, pillar,
chandelier, to stained glass window:
qui tollis peccata mundi.

The darkened sea of listeners
shrinks back, aside, murmurs
at a fearsome blast from
Boreas himself:
judex est venturus!

Tumultuous crescendo
and the movement ends. The players
catch their breath (the cellist
takes brief aim while
tightening his bow).

Now from out of the dark the bat
swings low again and by.
They look up, nod upon
his gentle turn and hear
Andante now, Johannes, andante!

Cassander's News

I am her brother, but because she speaks
overmuch, though truthfully, I too
am not believed.

Each word she speaks, I say, is well
in its judgment, but is one
of too many storming
across the plain like soldiers
of an army consuming its own feet.

They tramp towards us, dust
rising in clouds, obscuring their order
and the weapons they carry. They come on
blind as a plague, or revelation. I watch
in silence as so many fall

and leave no trace of the length
of their step while their loud cries keep
in the wind. For myself,
into what clear air is left I say
from time to time the mismatched ends

of phrases falling upon each other
hand to hand—dreams duel for an enemy's
kiss, after dark a lover scavenges
for a smile in the cool dirt—making no sense.

For now, then, I accept your doubt,
and spend my days wondering
about forgiveness. Later, perhaps,
will be a better time for truth.

Preliminary Sketches
The Counsel of Lascaux

I'll hunt no more the days of wind
and scent and running ridge and glade,
faint forest paths. Hunger
does not go home.

The only shelter still
is behind the ribs where timid creatures
go to hide, the narrow opening
in a raw cliff. I go there
like a child to the cave's
blind embrace.

Before my eyes were my own, I was told
of breezes stealing voices, of ghosts drooling
in icicles. Soon I knew what daybreak was and slant rain,
the chill blue mist of a clearing eve. Now
in the lengthening dark a passageway leads
to puzzling and dream. Pine knot fire takes me
to the catch of walls, scratching at stone, tracing creatures
pulsing through my hand
and a burnt stick.

Out of the stone arise aurochs
and antelope, galloping noiselessly. Shadows leap
into charcoal muscle, sinew and bone running red
in faint flame, leaving the dark.

Into the dawn of my drawing a horse also
wakes as I saw him once from above,
in smooth water, thinking he had fallen. But he only stood
alone in the shallows in windless twilight. Upside down
in reflection I sketch him, looking up -
where to find a hold for feet
pawing the clouds?

It is a riddle beyond begin
or sketch's end.

And I without imagining
step back into day, listen for the lisp
of tall grass. The thickets do not finish, the forest
empties into uneasy shade. I look
and go on, hunting, and questioning
the man I see from time to time
upside down at a water's edge,
when the wind is still.

Writer's Block

Words lie scattered, dismembered
by my bones. The cat's got my tongue
and took it up a tree, where his smile

guards the silence, slow food and a dark hole
no real cat can resist. We both know
that's where the truth is, and I

am the dark's bones. The leaves
ruffle like torn pages, but that smile
sees I keep the bait fresh, the flesh red

and inching crippled across the open,
asking only safe passage to destinations
indistinct and waiting for some word to fall

upon their deaf ears, a riddle no cat can catch.
So just return my tongue. I'll tell you a truth or two
to sate your mortal curiosity, but not mine.

Garden Dancing

What are you thinking,
Annabelle K., when you're thinking
what you think? Is it wings
or feet or color, taste
or touch or the warmth and fright
of one-two-three-one-two, tracking
the shy and trotting fox?

Is it a child's green night, gliding
and finding a garden of creatures
barbed together in a horned dance
to the bang and clatter of leaves?

For it was to that place
that the dragon of daybreak came,
claimed my child, stepping alone
and slow, and marvelously green
and striped, the caterpillar named Charger,
dazzle of boy and bee.

And there marched the chocolate turtle
named Champ, fresh from his squadron
of candies awake and straight through
your frail defenses, your sugar-dreamed
doubts of destiny and luck.

But while you're thinking
what it is you think, let turtle
match with caterpillar, dance
through taste, reel forward
on a green dream of sweet Champ
in Charger's charm.

For while the green and candy
dance together in the claim
of a child's cuddling faith, think
of melting chocolate and sweet, think
of spinning a hiding cocoon
for coming out with wings. Could it be
the match will turn to a different tune,
the partners change, you'll rename
Champ the Magic Monk, Charger
the Gossamer Vamp?

Because it was just like that
when Gramp first greened to Mabel,
dazzle of bird, bee and boy enough
to chew the sugar from the stalk,
the feigned ambush of dancing squared,
catching elbows seventy-nine swings, around
and again and do-si-do home.

Think of passing within reach,
yet slipping the barbs of touch,
like tidal crabs marching forward
sideways, scratching each other's
backs for a tickle of sun. Do-si-do-si-do,
crawl amphibious and slow, easy
to melt, late to find wings and less
for touch than back-to-back whispers
in garden lees. Grace the link
no less of hands than the fateful mix
and match of sugar leaves
and daybreak dreams, dragons
that hide, then fly.

So while you're thinking
what it is you think, it is
the glide, the quiet shuffle of mind
and feet, shy lope of foxes
trotting in that dim garden
toward creature warmth and fear
of a forest deeper of question, darker
of doubt. Bob and spin and
sweep and run and rush
forth backwards, clearing the way
for dancing and dreams.

And while you're thinking what it is,
you think, don't be fooled
by an eagle in blue, lost and forever
in his private sky, when you can have
both sweet and singing, greening feet
and dancing do-si-do-si-do
take-hands-for-home.

Curtain Call

for Rev. Bill

Backstage of his aging lights the sets
hang thin and breathless in the scaffolds,
their ropes loop along on random pegs,
gathering shadows.

Dismantled towns and the ageless fields
of record runs lean in pieces
on the invisible back wall, tranquil
in their long night.

As he takes an encore bow, he doesn't see
the audience long-since gone, nor as he acknowledges
the more capacious dark is he alone among
its distant stars.

He warms to the applause as memory's hands
rise yet again to cheer him home, see
the seasoned actor walk the spirit
to its multitudes.

The stage is his alone as he dreams again
a practiced narrative, famous lines
the absent audience has well since set to memory
and kept them young.

He wonders that it is without his leave,
for he so loved their listening and hears
no call to leave, as he is yet in earnest
of good words.

He knows the blackest wings of exit so symmetrical
to either side will fold about him feathery, the deference
of tiny theater lights will make a galaxy
of his familiar hall.

A janitor's shuffling quiet stirs fresh soliloquy
upon the favoring sea, a love trembling still
out of the dimming past, and as he's done and nods, he hears
the quiet clap.

Coming to Going

It was when I was five I found you
small in the picture frame beside our mother's bed.
You had already traveled your four months from the cradle
to memories in her pillow when she turned out the light
and closed her eyes. I have walked with you,
my brother, and walk with you now
toward the far reaches of becoming.

A dying friend tallies his arrival,
and elders on fragile threads like Christmas ornaments
hang in memory's door. Year and door close, and the tree
gives me its boughs to weave against the house
to keep out new snow, the north wind.

Imagining solves no mysteries now. I reckon
the numbers gone. Small pictures
flicker in my dim interiors, startle me
with star-lit ignitions to sing them a lullaby,
that they may draw me closer
to their sleep.

I sing beneath hearing
for a granddaughter, lace bonnet and silken hair,
oxygen tubes and ten month velvet cheek
upon my sixty-four year old shoulder
carrying her across a backyard,
too soon to play, too late to bless and keep her
from going away.

Are they so small and hurrying away
if not to bless and keep me looking
over my shoulder, like the living twin
waiting for the missing sister
to catch up?

They are far ahead, but I still come and go
without haste. I count properly and do not subtract,
and sing my little softness to them, making good
on a grown man's time, twinning absences,
catching up.

A Thrush's Song

A thrush still sings above its young tumbled to earth
for too little wing. He drinks more sky
and sings its blue with every feather quivering

for wind. But the wind has never known
that a yoke swimming in its perfect egg,
designing flight across a tiny sea,

is a bird already bursting with sun.
They school us early, don't they, my Daedalus;
the rhapsody we think we hear is a mind

ahead of itself and fooled by our own dizzying skill
into falling from the nest. We should have expected
no less: a child tempts a snug sun before he'll match wits

with a clever father, even if you tell him
that one forbidden thing is no more ominous
than another for threatening loveliness. But soon

your anguish rang through the stone cunning of your walls
all dumb with deceit when the haunting minor key
of a high bird struck your bones hollow, and you knew

Icarus was down. We have heard that narrow tremolo
forever, you and I, sweet with the similar tear we weep
when no stone marks a child's fall. Now again I listen:

the thrush is calling, longing for the young to linger yet
and sing before leaving without end.

January Thaw

It started to rain, then in no time
the ice on the brook turned brown.
Just January, I guess, and that makes me
another year older, all over again. Time
to act my age, maybe, if that means
going seventy plus is still going
like sixty, even though this time
the alarm rings faintly louder, as it does
each year, so it seems, just a hint maybe
my joints are out of time. Time
to check a friend's book of poems about winter
for details about cracks in the ice
and voices, wrinkles in faces and talk. Then comes
mud smudging the meadow, then a sly smile
smoothing a winter's first real good snowball.
But I'm not in a big hurry, and I'll find time
to say what I have to say for myself. It may not be
a postcard winter, but at least it'll be
more or less in time for this year's thaw
and one more January.

Meeting House

So white
beside a hayfield and a blue sky
whenever a northwest wind comes down
from Grafton Notch and blows the clouds away,
the old meeting house waits for its people as patiently
as barn and keep, still as the stone posts
and white-washed rails that hold a gentled earth
for souls come home.

We came today to mark
our final rest, bringing
four small corner stones
of granite—having but three,
I have broken the longest into two.

The farmer's son, apple cheeks, twenty and some,
stripling and lithe, a curly blond, hastens from his cares
for unkempt grass and headstones leaning
comfortably, lifts the latch, swings wide
the iron gate.

"Welcome," he says, and without another word
leads us to our square of ground. Looking up,
I watch him slip beneath the easy rise
of his father's vast and early fields

and hear yet the muffled clumping
of his rubber boots, sweet to the knee
with manure and dirt, across the fresh-turned earth
beyond where I can see.

Mining

Up from the mine where the canary
sang us a day to the picks and shovels
of worming men, we found the surface
as dusk came on.

And true enough, the sun was all but gone,
of a hurry to leave, too timid to stay
and dance, so black we were, the homely ones
gone down to dig,

dredged up ourselves out of the earth's
same dust, tongues blunt as our boots, blue
as our overalls stained with night, wondering
why a love in the breeze

would not forsake us to the rightful earnings
of sorrow. Gravity tugged at our stoop
falling just ahead of our feet
catching up,

as if going somewhere to start
a practiced hole in another darkness
where a canary might still sing
the favors of air.

So I walked italic, penning a cursive way
along the straight-lined streets among
the lamp-lit ghosts that finally slept at the margins
of fellow and town

and followed a country road that turned
ever and easily, taking footprints
into the reborn dark, invisible peripheries
where the tree tops thinned

and single things all hid. The shadows
breathed their slow off-center light, the dirt
warmed the soles of my feet
with a place to rest.

At the edge of the eye a farm
cuddled in the valley's crook,
its only square of light dim
and sufficient;

a flutter jumped up from a thicket,
flew over my road where the merciful trees
didn't swallow the shade, cage the air,
and I could lean

on the wind's shoulder, my hand balancing
on a hillside smelling green.
There was a stir in the herbal breeze,
hushed waves

carving the hard shore and men echoing
men, myself in their choir quarried and scrubbed,
singing from the soul's caverns
to the tempo of picks,

a shovel's phrase, the barrow's bass rumble
in its wheels sent out with all that was worked
and the little said into the precisely unknown.
We bore the dark,

the surface much the same, and dusk was waiting
at the ends of the west sea. We went on
where we were looking and sang
till the wind had ears.

                                                Wales, 2013

II.
Signs of Affection

Harley in Love

Miles of asphalt ride a moon-lit sea,
trim as a map through the curves

for gentle Harley stroking a landscape rounder
than round, creamy as a dream's beam of light

racing a luminous straight to a dot in the dark,
sure as a knot-hole in the night, one-eyed look

for a lover on pistons in fever, gears holding hands,
throttle in silk, a hundred and forty horse

Harley saddled up like Pegasus wooing a lady
who hides in the stars till dawn wakes up

and needs just another ordinary horse to pull a chariot
across everyone else's blue sky.

Love Song of a Resected Motorcyclist

I won't let a helmet cheat me of the wind
combing my hair, smoothing my cheeks,

when I can throttle up, roar and chase down
the softness waiting just up the road,

even if I have to show you my heart pulsing
naked in its cradle of bone, dumb

with loving but more manly than a fist
full of daisies. Then at least you'll know

there's a gift beyond reason, a loveliness
that forgives a brain its dying.

Harley Rides to the Altar

I'd give a rib for someone to love, and my heart
would burst through the opening to take her hand.
Creation was supposed to work that way

long ago, but she turned out to be
too beautiful, the heart swelled toward knowing,
and the opening was too small. It prowls now,

watching bars cut the sun to pieces, harden
the night. Once in a while I run
full tilt at the door in a dream raging

with sweetness, or more often chirp from a toy swing,
sit silent as a hawk hooded and tied
to an armored hand. No need to ask

why I won't let a helmet keep the wind from tangling
my hair, cooling a sunburned love-struck
smile with a sudden invitation to dance,

the spin you take down the road to where
the sky starts and your feet lift off the asphalt,
innards knock at their ribs trying to get out,

pistons croon through a smooth new corner
and I depart curve, earth and cage
at 110 forever, brainless maybe, but I've tried

everything else. Now a breeze leaves
the kiss of a split-second sun, and the heart
races straight for the altar, glad to exhale

once and for all. Looking down through blue light,
a priest in green lifts scalpel, clamp,
then saw from immaculate cloth because that rib

given long ago left the gap too tight.
He saws two more away and sees a heart
drumming its blood, bursting to get going.

The Longings of Stone

Small pink flowers bloom, their roots
in castle ruins. Invited to a lover's stroll,
a lady paused to squeeze his hand.

It's what a native stone awaits,
if he can just grow old, wrinkled,
abide the inching progress of frost,

the splitting wedges of sea wind,
the better to fit with kin for building
fortresses that will be left behind

in order that the master masonry decay
and crack to thinnest lips for sipping rain
and being comfortable with clouds.

A seed will happen by, if the breeze stays,
and take his stiff, cold arm. In time enough
he'll breathe in the tendrils' green embrace

and then flowers blooming
small and pink.

Thin Air

I married the thin air
into which you vanished.

Many others were in attendance
singing a paper song,

open-mouthed in choir along the edges
of their breathless universe.

You joined them there and I promise
to cherish and obey the thin air

until I am more certain of what disappearing
requires of a man and if that

is better known as love. Trappings of self
shall be invisible, and talk

not given up not given at all, for the thin air
conceals what is to say

until the body hollowed, bridged and strung receives
the bow of an errant hand.

Then pale sound rises up and travels
among us like mist

wishing to be gone except to ask for a small
portion of that thin air,

knowing, like you, a word alone
would be so kind.

As Pyramus to Thisbe

Put two fingers to your lips
as I put two to mine.

Together let them be the wall
with a narrow crack our breaths

push through to meet softly against each other
in the middle of where, forbidden unjustly,

distance keeps impossible lovers
helpless in the warm embrace

of their ageless complicity.

Adam's Lament

I met a fool in the woods
and was alone.

The voice at my side
slipped away to the birds and their small talk
lost in the clouds,

while out on the forest floor blossoms
swoon in the perfume of spruce, pick partners
quicker than feet, and the woods
won't tell of it.

Will ever a word return, softly said
and round? It's a fool's best question, all ear,
imagining dancing in the chill quiet
of this place.

Eve Replying

I didn't just vanish
from your side, Adam. A silence in me
wanted me back. Before we were cast out,
too many things were left unsaid. Nor could I really guess
what to listen for. You certainly never said much,
but you had the ears of a hunter
for the softest rustle in the woods, the wind shift
when the quiet spills into itself so suddenly,
it fills you to bursting. Then the sky
comes inside you and you feel
terribly alone. It was not seldom
that you went off hunting voices
by yourself.

But don't imagine I left you
for lack of conversation. We were both ashamed,
looking back over our shoulders, supposing
we should know why because of an apple,
that confusing incident at the tree. All I did was
pick the closest one. You took a bite and stared at me
startled, as if I had surprised you with some
peculiar truth. I just thought
you looked hungry.

Nor was I walking beside you
just because you gave me
one of your ribs. I gave you my hand
and loved you holding it. The apple
didn't teach us that.

I just had to come back
for another look. It's not as perfect
as the story told it. That was to make it
look like our own fault. Actually,
the Garden needs real tidying up. I turn the earth
around raspberries, level them up,
so they can drink with dry feet. It's rich ground, Adam,
dark and reeking with sweetness in the roots,
pale shoots, and birds come flirting
to the puddles, coy to the rowdy gusts, gossipy
as leaves, boisterous as branches flexing their muscles
in the wind, come close if I don't look at them. I dig
and the dirt flies, my hair races like rain, my shirt
wrings fragrant as old wood, mud squeezes between my toes,
my fingernails, goes halfway up my arms.
I put on the Garden's mess
like fresh clothes.

The quiet runs deep
in the Garden, Adam, but it rumors
if you wait for your ears. After a time it rolled
on my tongue into *raspberry*, *plum*
and *purple* suddenly, suddenly *hyacinth* and *lily*, *lupine*,
round, lemony licks of words. And suddenly I also said
turnip, and it made me smile, as if a voice had just told me
a secret, or a funny story. Still, it's hard to know
if you really know, for words aren't round
or red enough for an apple, and too pale
to paint the flowers brushing our knees
as we trudged along not knowing why
or what to say.

You must have guessed the apple
wasn't quite like the story had it. Maybe that's why
you always ran until your heartbeat
drowned out birdsong, the wind's howl, the drums
of rain. You were hunting voices, so you
gave your quiet its own time back. Back here in the Garden
I am finding my quiet too, with its own taste
in my words. And I'm no longer frightened
that I might lose myself in someone else's
important story.

Can you hear my silence, Adam,
smooth as milk and cool to your lips?
And if in the weakening light of a tangled wood
you stumble now and then, think of fingers
linked, rock to rock across a stream, wet feet
up through a meadow steaming dry
among daisies and a yellow forenoon sun
enough to make the very quiet
speak.

From Jane

Tarzan, darling,
seventy years old may not seem
right. But not all justice
is at the end of a vine, or every
battle hymn the cry
of an ape.

      I love you for those things, also
your beach bronze and naked
eyes, and they have made
our country great.

          But don't be frightened,
my pet, let those oblong pectorals
slip away between your ribs, let your bulbous
gastrocs rise and hide behind
your knees.

      All that was just too much
for cuddling, and cuddling
was the justice I sought. Despite the moon,
your python biceps scared me
to stone.....you were always so
dangerous.

      Now I know
you're really there. Muscles are softer,
but bones tell the truth. I love your ribs,
your knees, your faltering voice: they hold
great secrets. Now I can tell.

      Take my hand,
let's walk in the park
this very morning. I don't want
to know your secrets, just that
they are there. Your quiet passing by
with me will be enough.

      We will walk and watch
the skim of birds, the quickening
glance and the giggle of girls, listen
to the flutes of children, the trumpeting
of young men.

     Tarzan, darling, the jungle
is so fine!

Tarzan Replying

Dear Jane,
I appreciate your sympathies
on my turning seventy, more or less, and your invitation
to come down from my tree to walk in the park with you.
Your name still rings from anywhere I know — muscles
are no defense for that — and I'm certainly no longer
the swinger I was, though I do practice some
most days.

      But a stroll in a park would be too frightening,
holding hands where strangers would look
and make me feel more naked than the two of us up here
on our bed of boughs and soft leaves with nothing on
but the moon, his eyes closed
but smiling anyway.

      Remember when
the wind was still, our high limbs kept moving back
and forth in that odd rhythm, as if the earth itself
was breathing, its huge chest rising and
falling, rocking us snug
in arms of soft air?

      That may have been my imagination,
I know, and you're the only witness to how strangely
I behaved for loving you so. I had a lot to say about it,
but sigh and whistle and roar were all I could
come up with. The whole forest understood though,
you'll remember, because they all roared back in chorus,
howling their heavenly serenade.

Love must make its own
peculiar music, and you need an ear for it. I sensed
what was happening right off, even though I couldn't
understand it, and probably never will. Besides, you were full
of voices, and understanding had nothing to do
with any of them.

    You were all gift, surely blessèd, as they say,
but we both know receiving is harder. For one thing,
when you were making sense, I just couldn't
understand you. The rows of colored words tangled
on your lips, and your eyes
stole them away.

    Then your letter arrived,
straight lines on a blank page, big letters to start,
dots to stop, and all I could think of was my town as a boy,
with its streets and corners, signs and lights telling me to go
or stop. "Caution" seemed to say don't do either, and "Wait"
was a total mystery. I just had never seen a decent fence
I didn't have to jump over, and it was people
that barked; the dogs just wagged their tails.

    You said it yourself, there are secrets we have, and
they're not to know. I'm glad you have some too,
and I'm just as glad not knowing what they are. In a way
they made you speechless, vast as night, bigger than yourself.
You also said, of course, that you liked to cuddle
to feel small enough again and fit into one place.

                But cuddle justice
isn't on a park bench, watching children play. The flutes
and trumpets you hear followed you there from the forest
because they wanted you back. They'd rather be lifting
smells of ripe earth up through the trees, or gathering stars
full of stories down to the high branches, where you're never
quite sure if you're walking or flying. You just get along
with everybody and enjoy their bewitching voices.
The talking and the singing aren't much different,
and they touch just lightly on the jungle's
delicious quiet.

                I'm not going to say
you'll find me all that delicious, but I'm certainly
not as dangerous as you claim to remember. I'm less muscle
and more leopard skin; less to cover up and more covering it.
So I'm hardly a threat, although my legs do stay lean,
my temperature above average, and my shoulder
still shows the soft curve
of your cheek.

I've also mended the ladder, in case
you were wondering.

Dressing for Spring's Wedding

Lest your body feel bereft of proper attire,
the velvet season has been extended
through April to May and maybe June,
if you have nothing in silk,

for velvet still suits the violet cuddle
of lilacs slipping from damp shadows
into furtive perfume, and silk
will wait the other month

till iris bloom, tongues hanging
breathless and purple, limp with kissing
the wind's smooth skin in a garden
of themselves, not a soul in attendance.

Clericus at Dusk
a vagabond scholar's journal of the 12th century

Here I sit the end of day, faint-eyed
from the assaults of loveliness and still
not certain whether I am recalling or composing
these sweet apostate joys in the service of agapé
or eros. I mark my words, some dipped, I admit,
in pagan ink, onto a palimpsest of prayer and pledge,
the offerings of kisses taken up for night
in its own eternal house.

My notes are slow, and dreams interfere,
but I follow my trimmed quill doggedly
along its way to where love takes the truth
beyond all reason. No garrulous believer
in luke-warm hospitality, I have always had
better than average legs, a lean stomach, and camp well
beside a country road.

Now at respite in a drafty traveler's shed
the geography of spirit spreads forth
its run of blues, commotions of green, the amber hue
of slender arms beyond all dust or the humble tools
of an arthritic scribe. Yet my knuckles
lately swelled to tender hammers still set
and drive their good consonants like sleek nails
and sundry winded vowels too voluptuous
for a reticent world.

I gain advantage at the page, lengthen my arm
like a divine lever to multiply my innards' burn,
consume the regulations of pen and ink, the fleeting mercy
of fine sand, blotting the ink, timing the days.

Oh, strike my words their length
into this wooden world, even when its mystery stays home
in the hard, green silence where it begins, beyond all creation
but its own.

So hard it is and vain perhaps
to fashion a proper chronicle of prayer,
a delicate wrist, devotion broken
by a smile, gray eyes, even
with the most painstaking joinery. I nail each word
as firmly as the matter takes, then just bend the rest over,
flush with the surface of things, where I first
and forever loved as much a lady and a lily
of the field, lady slippers in the breathless pine forest
and a lady in slippers as well,
all God's work.

I am hungry now
and the evening chills. But I'll sleep young
knowing that tomorrow will again provide
His work to do.

The Shade Nearby
(one of the Cleric's poems)

Let us kiss in the shade
and shelter of the cemetery trees
among the tipsy stones and drink
too much of fall's fermented breeze.

We'll say the names of places
known to hugs but secrets
still have kept and race
faint paths to hiding

and release from thoughts
of never dying, waiting thus
forever. Springs would come
too surely and excuse our patience

with the strangeness come of gifts
for timid lips that gently grace
our few jeweled minutes
among the watchful graves.

Poetry Is the Wolf

If you wonder that I approach you
with some hesitation, it is not for lack
of desire.

Stealth hides a shyness of heart not shared
by my words.

But neither would my words be so crass
as to walk straight to the matter like any dog
to meat.

The wolf in them is still courtly, circling in with lilting step
to get acquainted first with what it is
he longs for,

then loping warily along to one another's step
until the note of harm becomes familiar rhythm, matching
unsaid word for word said, the tooth and tongue
of hunger.

But if you slip away from a tangle of arms, I'll howl
till the moon can catch you waiting
in a dream.

Solitude

Spinster night likes ardent talk,
but this staring at stars numbs the tongue,
and constellations crowd the spaces out. A single star
falls fiery, and a stranger cries "look!"

from the bleacher seat we apparently share.
True enough, the field of light out there is one
of the dark's charms. I see the small figure in white
race the corners of a diamond far away.

But I'll speak up when my toes get to dig
in the fresh dirt, where usual joy sends a leaf
bursting from its limb more lovely
than the dove from a magician's sleeve.

So I would caution solitude against taking
liberties, for there comes a distance which belief
will not span, even if her loveliest shadow says
if I would just step forth upon a bridge not there,

she will take my hand. Love may make
a fool, but I'll tell you I'm not out here
in the dark to behold your flutter of distant
lights or sign up for a celestial team.

Say something softly,
on my side of the night, and maybe
we'll go for a short walk.

Parsing Her Quiet

I'm most of what I'm not, for love
is the maker of solitudes.

Planted in the ground, a parent's flag, I flutter
among folk who welcome once but thinly
to the perfect silence of their sky.

It is their church whose Word countenances
but one Beginning, and we are the loose change
fingered in the dark bottoms of worn pockets.

Upon her lap I watch her slender hands hold back
unpracticed talk, lest a tremor in the earth blossom
into words too fragile and exquisite.

I've also watched her hands both fold hard
around a pitchfork firm stuck in the ground like a brace
staking a sapling apple tree on an exposed hillside.

She does not breathe the air of words, and sunlight
splits the glance of those most hazel-green of eyes
that watch me fluttering in the sky's tug.

Tide Walker

Days and nights I nudge the shore, catching at the arms
of seaweed indifferent with desire,

tread water without end, toe down for doubtful ledge,
eyeing the dry stone, kissed

by innocent fishes and the ebb's caresses cured in salt,
even as the wind stirs fresh libido

in the tide's hug, the ruthless peace a shore keeps
to itself. But silence need not fear

its coy wishes, for the shortest of my breaths
will find a thread to string a necklace

of bright syllables that delight replying, as pebbles
make a ring for the damp sand,

nor will the sea caught up in a moon's eye complain
if what is left of a trunk and limb

lingers on the warm bedrock and dries
to live bone, the wind's ruin left behind

as the tide ebbs.

Carnal Knowledge

I want to see the wounds I've dealt
and show the scars I wear. I would point out
the faintest outline of a footprint
on the left side of my chest, a misshapen
right ear, the cuts where new body parts
went in for those worn down
by heat and mileage—an eye for the one
that blurred the truth, a gland playing host
to uninvited guests, a hip from the swift, relentless chase
of exquisite phantoms, mesh for a stomach
lost to battle. I'd have you notice
my gait occasionally reticent with its sum
of trivial retributions, my nose
gone west like a weather vane
put out of joint by a furious storm.

Look at me, I'm not exactly
the furry prize you get for knocking over
a pyramid of wooden bottles at the fair,
nor the sinewy giant in the mind of the damsel
planning her distress. But I do not
hide nor blush, and I will heed
each stroke you have endured until you too
no longer blush.

Mario's First Son

My wife was a beautiful skater,
fleet as a breeze and
sharp as cold. She
carved my eyes.

She skimmed our summer
in her skiff like a bird.
About the island the water
was smooth, not a nerve of wind.

She was at me like a leaf
tossed by to tag, and I
was it with tickle. The kiss
knocked so gently at my door,
I opened.

Black her hair and waved, her eyes,
her shadows cradled
the dark. The island woke
the child away.

She buried the child
in her middle, rocking
a jewel in her velvet ice, trim
as the island stone and round.

Her breath caught, her lips
tore the echo
from a cove. A child
roared back to her arms.

The seventh, the one
dark son. My wife was
a beautiful skater, curved
the wind, carved
him from me
with a kiss.

Of Love and Baked Apples

Where is it, the core
I mean? Taken out first in this
special recipe, savory, personal,
done up brown,
as they say.

The apple, my example, baked,
seasoned, sweet, cinnamon
and sugar, a little wrinkled
but full of wisdom,
it is said.

But the core is gone,
you see (or rather
you don't see), from which the knowing
and all blessings flow, once the seasoning,
basting and tasting start, when it is clear
I do not well resist
my hunger.

But I hasten to say
I do not love well either, when all
is said and done, short of further
information.

Keep the core in
next time. After the seasoning
and sweet, bits and seeds
keep a delicacy in things
left over, almost said.

Travelogue

With solemn gentleness my fingers travel
the vast hollow of your stomach stretching lambent
among shadows threatening to flee.

Mists from forgotten mountains arrive
to claim my arm, though I lend an ear
to the growling of a ravenous sea.

I'm lost in your dozen landscapes, your wilderness
of light, the eyeless sky, feral dark. In the shelter
of your chin a shade conceals your half-smile's

sweet attack. A kiss concedes, but not the path
that shows an index finger to the reaches
of your clavicle, smooth as marble, then

to the restless precision of your backbone so beloved
of ancients as the ladder up to heaven that they visited
at personal times of night, ardent heroes underway

to their constellations' dim eternity, though after a time
inclined to take the ladder down at dawn to refresh themselves
on mortal joys. And none too soon, for behind your knee

a velvet cave you've never seen has stopped all thought
and bids my fingers just refreshed to journey on alone,
accept the ivory invitation of your ankle, the winking

of your toe that sings a siren's song. Should you be mystified
I move about you like a lost rain, causing sudden
moisture, unaccustomed warmth, don't be alarmed.

I'll soon come to the rib I'm missing, your share
of me. You've doubtless noticed I know little
of geography but a little something more of joy,

and only one of us, after all, needs to know the lay
of the land in the mute openings of imagination
where we travel on and on until our ribs fit.

A Lesson in Love at the County Fair

Step right up and visit, dear lovers,
with Princess Zamora, peripatetic gypsy gymnast
just arrived from distant steppe and clime, gifted
in flights elliptical that make the parallel bars
vanish as her smile slips right behind your very eyes!

And with myself, but briefly in from outer space,
Redoubtable Luigi, architect of peripheries
and periphrastic adventure, deft afoot
with centers of gravity just for the taking
on orbital junkets, the perfectly celestial spin!

Watch us do a pas de deux for
you, dear people, launching delicate and
limber from the parallels too innocent to
ever touch. Alas, they seldom try, but you will
see the trick's to swing so gallantly, the

world goes nicely upside down beyond the
tethers of geometry or bars keeping you no
longer but to one another flying in the cloudless
air like birds in very personal formation. See it

for yourself, and then invite your loved one
to a feathered dream!

Waltzing in a Parking Lot

Left two three, right two three, turn again, waltz
in a parking lot square cut and flat, dancing

elliptical shadows across the smooth snow. All the cars
have gone elsewhere, but elsewhere is waiting right here,

vacant and fair for the waltzing a tangle
of arms and ephemeral steps to a riddle of threes,

rhythms unsung but a song like the curious wind
that spirals us up out of yesterday's ashes, you say,

while I hear the clicks of the tumblers a thief
ever so furtively turns two three, right two three,

running the spindles to riches unknown, if only
this hour, a minute, a split-second kiss on the silk

of a softening eye, two three, right two, a bolt is thrown back
on a darkness inside, and we see now that more than this

will not be there beyond waltzing in a parking lot
toe to your toe in the narrowing sun of an afternoon woods,

face to face at arms' length from primeval moments alone
when more than this that would never be there began,

dancing our tangents to earth's endless curve
in a parking lot empty and we two alone.

Shards

I

You went to your sea, I
to mine, for it had come summer,
and we had danced our once
far inland on the high west plain
through an evening in May.

Beneath a big screen rodeo, the kick
and snort of storming broncs,
a stereophonic cowboy stirred his dusty
heart to the beat of pity
and hooves, crooning his ache
to moon and stars.

Every same song died
on every tongue that night. A dozen times
the winded, beat-down tune drove us
like flotsam across the polished floor, eddying
eye to eye, running on
to still remembrance in the catch
of shadow steps, dipping feet, knees
quaking in the chill wash
of fiddles.

II

Now at my Maine shore, the August tide
chews on upstream stone, scoured,
rubbed and rounded to pebbles,
ebbs with its random catch,

and I wade the shallows to a sandbar, water-swept
for the pipers' step and mine, forward now,
then back from the surf running rich
in its rush, poor
in its fill.

The crash of water and the wind's ache
drum on the ripples of a backstream
breaking at the piper's call, and our tracks
cannot outlive the sudden fill
of silence.

The lathered waves charge in
to the wind's whip, tossing down
each errant, primitive call,
vessel and voice broken, stolen
for shards.

III

There, at your Pacific shore, have you asked
the creatures dance with you? Have they answered
the urgent note the waves throw down
onto the shocked sand? Have you counted
to their step and matched their measure
of shadow step and kick, forward
and back of the sea spill? Does your sea
vanish upwind, swelling in full aphasic chorus
with your secrets, bartering beach for
some passing touch, some mute
consensus, alien and eloquent
as driftwood?

It is written in the history
of this Popham shore that an Abnaki man
warned how the talkless water steals
our messages holding a wish, daring, love,
a brave sadness. He returns in secret, so you
will not see him leave his reply, your once own words
cut and tumbled smooth, made strange
and without hands, sea glass, signs bent
and bleached into wood, necklaces
of pebbles.

Have you been suspicious enough
of this man, turned back
to the inland shelter talk
of trees, their lips pouting
with hush, their damp limbs sweet
with shadows?

IV

Not knowing how words may dwell
in distance, I will say to you only:
I went to my sea, found you
away at yours and have turned, shivering
and wordy from the salt spray, the stench
of mud, the frail skitter
of man and bird along the polished
miles of sand.

I will say to you I have gone
inland now, gathering a bouquet
of hack, reed and grass, breathed in
its dusty green as pale and fragrant
as your sage, and simply speak the voices
pounding in my ear.
Perhaps this gentled air will rush
upon your window, open it, steal forth
from the billowed curtain and leave
some faint, some
cut and tumbled word
beside your pillow.

Rain on the Mountain

I went looking on the mountain
alone. I thought of asking you along,
but there was a hard rain. On a day like this
the clouds lie down with ridge and gap, each nudging breeze
the footfall of a bird upon a limb. I breathe my steam
into the air for thin warmth

and the nodding of celibate trees, the chill
courtesies of wind that takes one leaf
after the other and carries it off
to its own infinite desire. Can a wind pleasure
in the catch of leaves, scattering heart beats
across the forest floor? Does my subtraction
fill the lush requirements of some
impending beauty?

Perhaps you will collect a few
of the more brightly colored leaves and float them
in a dish, see the slight veins, the lifting edges,
smooth skin. Perhaps you will consider them
small poems and give one or the other
back to me, and I will recall them
as I do the immaculate tenderness
of the daddy long-legs stepping along
my bare shoulder, down my arm.

Looking for Dorothy

You came in the mail in a shoebox
full of cousins, mothers, a century of men
and squinty boys who would beget their daughters
and more boys, who would grow tall, lovely,
combed at last and old. Some sit stiffly,
others stand. No air stirs in the studio
to move a wisp of hair or help a smile bloom
sly, a wrinkled wink or eye caught closed.
The hooded camera stops the wind till
all are settled, bored and staring blankly back,
a choir ready to sing forth
from the family mists.

A frame apart, you gently mock
the laced and rigid relatives, sing out
your silence right at me so lenient and soft
with oldest rumor of delight
to undo breath and time.

You also see me looking back,
and I will fairly claim to just those eyes
your vale of tears will never be as stormed
as mine who loves you suddenly,
wrestles the days with memory
to find you and will fail.

My rival is no man of arms
and has no name, but he sleeps
with one eye open lest I break and enter history
or play the child who climbs among the family branches,
old man and fool for finding you have broken off and gone.
And when I wake from dreams of nods, your answers
modest and melodic, still you leave me
jealous of the ease in anonymity
behind your smile.

And now your eyes abide behind my own
and beyond seeing, even while I know
you won't forsake your short cut hair swept down
across those eyes set brown within
still brows, finest lashes, nose falling slim
above soft lips that pillow slender syllables
asleep inside.

But I hear them, your request
I leave you to beauty on the safer side
of idle sadness and desire
and call off the search.

Forgiving

I cannot say the words
that stir along my tongue or catch your fingers
floating on the liquid air before you know
that I forgive you if you do not
find joy in this

and beg your pardon too of me
who burdens you with your refusal
of such unruly energy too great to be contained
or governed by a solitary man, should he transgress
even unto gentleness. Into that omission rushes
the unfinished sentence, furtive
half embrace, witness only
that this vessel is too small
and too full.

May the urge to give
what will be and cannot be given
be forgiven, though it be an insufficient mercy
upon love burst out among us without regard
for names or the little strength of men.
I do not know how this drink gathered
in this cup, mine and not mine,
that will revel so
to running over

when I meet you in the absent reason
for a sudden rain, in the taste of a spring
come cold from underground.

Tea Ceremony

I am making two cups
of mint tea. One is for you, the other
for me. Your cup
is smaller, but it is
just as full.

Perhaps you will drink your cup, its mint
with honey, as you like it,
its simple warmth. But if
you do not want this cup, it
will not be wasted. I will drink
of its emptiness, drop
for drop.

A Diary of Sighs

Something wonderful
is over. The peace of the sky
has wandered off, the wind
has stopped looking.

Day's plough has turned
the calendar's sod. The seed
in friable dirt trembles
to the season's jig.

Husbandry extends itself
to ephemeral things, the drift
of shade, leaves consorting
with a fickle rain.

A crow on a bare branch
feigns sweet argument,
fooling no one. His kill
will have to die first
on its own.

Nothing is amiss.
The heart rehearses
its trochaic thump, alone
in a cave of bone
long lost to ears.

A girl child walks her distant way
learning to whistle.

The Musical Evening of Sister Elizabeth

Sister Elizabeth, pale as pearl,
looks down upon the nave, and there
she sees the pianist come forth, aglow
in white and tails, descending
in a beam of light.

In the cathedral become concert hall
he looks aloft, closes his eyes and ears
around the music, as his lean athletic fingers
run caressingly, mysterious and crossing in
and over harmonies disarming and divine. The runs
and the disruptions syncopate their messages of soul
unheard before in monotones of prayer, while the trills
and tremolos discover other chords inside Elizabeth,
a tidal surge of music tugged elliptical
by pianist and moon.

As he sways upon more slowly
measured pace, the notes each gather, catch
and curl around his touch, or suddenly racing onward spring
upon the lithe, the supple grace of hands floating
on the muscled waves of music perilous with passion,
with near emergency.

Sitting not far distant in row three,
Elizabeth must close her eyes to rise
inside the holy vault and feel the comfort
of forgiveness smooth the vestments
of her soul, even as she thrills to the tangle
of allegros, tintinnabulations, trembles
to the rhythmic innuendo of his
insistent song, his rippling melody.

Retreating in diminuendo, the playing sinks now
and is gone. She prays, for from on high illuminated notes
have drifted down as with a laying on of hands
to tease her very spine with subtlest adagio and gentle fifth,
and in the mercy of the dark she opens
into beatific smile for Chopin
and his polonaise.

Immaculate Conception
Joseph's Song of Loneliness and Thanksgiving

How could I play so Joseph, second fiddle
to a mystery Maker, you asked, while night
and nighty filled up more
with His absence than
with me. Still, I'm donkey enough
to suffer a good riding, day
or night, with stoic smile. Let's at least admit
I got you in the mood; those weren't exactly
hooves I played up and down your spine
enough to make you start to hum something
I couldn't quite understand and
close your eyes. Where were you then? Yet
I should admit as well that beyond that
ivory back and flanks like damp soap
I tried on some closed eyes
and began to hum rather inco-
herently myself.
                    "Oh, God!"
I shouted (at a sudden lurch
in the road)....enough to wake you smiling
down at me like a stalk of wheat bent
by a fresh breeze, when all through the trip
from nibble to gallop, however and
very close we were, we were each
just as rather absent.
                Then you too burst out,
"Oh, God!" and I'll bet it was Him coming
among us, as we did, oh dear, gallop there
a little.
                Since then,

                                              continued

far from going into things, love and divinity
in particular, with eyes open, I just
drift in and out of the whole undertaking
so wonderfully full of feather fingers,
birds and bushes, galloping a little here
and there, like the good ass that brought you home
for some other Guy.
                  Nevertheless, I'd have to say
for Him, He had a nice way
of coming among us indeed and
very close when we were each and
the other as well, because we were
certainly not ourselves and more
beside ourselves than beside each other. No wonder
something marvelous came of it.
                          And then
the night was over, enough indeed
and so very close, and I wouldn't really know
what else to say but
"Oh God!" and be so glad
to find Somebody handy who can
keep a clear head at times
like that.

III.
A Fellowship of Strangers

The Choir Director Has a Talk With God

I don't say much. Maybe I'm a little afraid
of what I know. I've been clear as I could be,
once or twice, face to face, but they
just look off the other way, as if
they don't see me. Now I keep to the singing.
It's just easier if you don't get too close
to a word, or if you just stay out of sight all together,
like an animal safe in his eye and ear.
                                        That's why
I came here to the choir loft. It's my tree line. I can see
what comes and goes in the meadow, sort of
like You, I suppose, and catch the words
that fence the edges, although they're shy
in the forenoon sun, as if the truth is too harsh
to say out loud.
                So I don't blame folks
gone quiet. I have my own reasons for being shy,
but I sound my baritone when the choir stands
with these lank souls come to forest and field,
time before dawn, faces carved from stump and stone, hair
combed hard around the ears chilled blue with listening
for news, the chapter and verse of a second cutting
set aside to dry with a season's tools and talk.
                                                For my part,
I dust off prayer book and hymnal, sweep the floor.
And having some idea how You put us together, I go down
first thing Sunday morning and light the furnace fire;
cold drafts enough feed on a heart, they don't
need our ankles too.

Now the pews begin their creaking, doing what they can
to settle a week's portion of pain. Caved eyes ease
in the stain-glass shade. They can't see me,
but I'm on the job, like You, I guess, and I don't
have to look long or far to know victory
is out of the question. You must have made a truce
between days of dust and the brush of wings
that sweep it up, between a world of sighs
and angel song. Maybe it was then
that mercy occurred to You,
or love.

Whatever it was, I don't bother much
if they don't round off all the words, for a word
is just a cup of sound, and the cup that runs over
is already singing. At least it's nice to think so
as we sing our hymns, four verses every one,
so rhyme and melody have time to beat their wings
and cool a mouth of clay sore parched for words.
                                    The silence
doesn't seem so shy when sung by souls
who come to their small dawns unseen, though You
surely see and see that we are not so sure because we
only feel the rough contours of the field we mow
or the wind muttering the faint beginnings of a hymn, as You
apparently intend, looking out from Your loft and singing
to startled ears and yet another day.

Winter Talk

As surely as old men gather
in their morning coffee corner to look
through frosted windows upon the passing world
and watch a winsome mother and her bundled son
glide by, that often they begin to talk their way
into this next vacant day.

They will love the mother and the son again
for the embers aching still this young
gray-headed morn when generations
fighting to love best jump
their many numbered bones.

How can any one of them escape so many years
of bursting, now their bones invite soft flesh
no longer, when they have long since
loved the fur off the stuffed rabbit
and know to cherish yet a threadbare friend?

So they love both her and him, each every day
as if for the first time, leaping
through the prison of their brittle bones to doing time
and talk once more. For mother and son
pass by their sudden flex, their quickening blood

and all the things an old man knows for them
of growing up forever in the thrall of sweetness,
the hug of morning's chill.

Twilight of Barns

Ethan Fellows forever praised
the holy days of building barns and then
became the praise, tall in the plum-gray dusk.
Post and beam hung true to tenon and peg,
flew from their toes across the hay-filled,
sweet-dried sky.

Miles above the floor and its knots
like polished stones, the cupola opened
a cooing place for doves drifted home
from the clouds.

Then the three day blizzard of '86
brought down the sky and put the issue of heaven
to rest. His barn was long on hold
but fine of rib and ridge and buckled
beneath the fat snow.

When in the spring a wondrous light
climbed through the parted roof and down
the laddered dust, Ethan gazed up in full regret
of all frail purpose warming his threadbare breast.
Patience thinned his bones. His voice stumbled
in his praise as in his prayer.

Two days Rachel knew
the rope lay draped in the crook of his arm, tangled
as his furied hair, while Ethan stared the sprung rafters still
above a splintered earth. With the dull crunch
deep in that winter night he had come to know
the farm would not be done but first undone
by a season only he could finish. A true hurt
must not heal cheaply.

From the drop of his lashes opening slowly
to her eyes, from the turn in timorous reverence
toward the cupola fallen from heaven at his feet,
Rachel learned his choice of a doubtless way. She
returned to her kitchen and gave Ethan back to himself.
In that moment of abundance
the rafter held.

Veterans' Day

When he was a boy, he said, wild grapes grew
on the stone wall nearly buried now beneath the matted grass
and flowers gone to seed in the dog-hair brush,
the pine shadows half way up the hill.

In the days before the Great War they grew,
and afterwards the wall and the grapes were there
to talk about with fellow veterans when they met
on their day of the year and had their picture taken
for the newspaper. They gather still, bearded
and squat, bald with time's burdens but smiling
with what they know.

If you look, you know a few, and two are young
who wear the latest uniform instead of overalls
and Legion cap. A few are missing alive
from a war far away in the East. They march
out of range of flag or photo and are still missing
on Veterans' Day, although we know them
and their whereabouts.

Once they also knew
the secret places of wild grapes, but memory
did not return from battle, and they were taken prisoner
when they came home, given stones
to bear along the dim path toward a distant rim of light.
We lift their eyes a little if we pray for them
from time to time and say aloud
it is not their pride they suffer
but ours.

First, hear their argument: We are the prisoners
not taken with our brothers into the arms
of mercy's gentler death. We wander
alone on Purgatory's mountain,
carrying our stones. We know of no gift
found wild, no day
that is ours.

Now let us bring them back from the mountain
to their primeval field, take up their stones,
as farmers with farmers lifting stones
from a pasture's troubled back, fit them
to the wall at the hard boundaries of self
made beautiful once more in the trim geometry
of redemption, the sweaty physics
of common soul.

And let the wall revive its remnant soil
in the catch of another season's leaves and twigs
and seeds sown by the wind and the flight of birds,
preparing memory's renewal, the return
of wild grapes.

Bailey's Small Engine Repair
Timer Bailey, prop.

Heaven only knows what Timer knew
to muster all the ticking of the days
towards quitting time
and going home.

And nobody would have called him Timer
had we not known that he kept every tick,
both his and ours, as sharp as chain saw teeth, precisely spaced
and comfortable among the gears nearby and flywheels,
belts and bearings schooled to music
soothing to small engines, which is to say
he chose to look after the likes
of most of us.

We marveled though he did not.
Rehearsing his and our repose near noon,
he dozed a well-conducted nap among the cloud-like cushions
of his armchair tucked amidst eternal shelves
of spare parts anyone could ever need for doctoring
the myriad frail items of creation destined
to wear out.

Mozart played in dusty light from high above
the chair where Timer slept, his eyes aloft in peace,
his smile content with all the grime
and grease he generously took upon himself
and generously dispensed to make things calmly spin,
till, cut or roll, mow
or turn the earth.

He also must have had a good idea
that Heaven only would decide
the number of his days: spaced exactly, timed
and tuned to angels' music and the Lord's law
of motors slowing down
beyond repair.

A Finnish Ice Lantern
Rudi Honkala's Will

Of my life of ice
and snow, I can tell you
this much.

The water in a bucket
will not freeze
totally. A small center resists
even the fiercest cold. A night,
a day and a night
will do.

Warm the bucket's surface
a little. Turn it
upside down. The ice
drops out, still thin
at its top. Break a hole there,
enough for a hand,
and let the water
run out.

In the hole
place
a candle.

Toshi's Reluctant Mushrooms

I fix a Toyota, and it runs
like a race car, hums along softly
like my daughter's violin. Shiitake mushrooms
wait for lightning.

They rest in their oak racks
in a dark shed. I wet the air,
go away, and wait. Thunder comes, lightning
cracks, wakes them up. Then
they grow.

If dry days stay too long, I go
late in the afternoon, when storms come, and bang
two or three times on the racks
with my pipe.

Then they grow too.

Walking Dawn

Simon Cross did not want dawn
to leave its home alone, rising from the night
like a solitary farmer crossing a pitch dark yard
to wake his barn, for Simon was like enough alone
in his dark, and the bleary eye of dawn
is a found friend he summons to rise
and be walking. Big in his mind,
it has no name to forget,
and he forgets many.

But names he doesn't need, for he will ask
as simply as the day dries familiar leaves
all over again with an early breeze, arranges faces
at pale windows just as he starts out from the family fields
to knock on dawn's doors and trace with practiced footsteps
his persistent and elusive self.

As he walks he counts
the morning's multitude of chores, dim squares of light
and the murmur of milking, the sweet breath
of cut hay, a chorus of cows extolling
new grass. Mist exits a meadow
like ghostly movie-goers as the dark retreats,
or so it seems to him, like threadbare sheets
that start at his approach and hurry the last
of local sleep into the arms of trees.

So Simon goes, at peace in the perfection
of woodpiles, the cinnamon air around the bakery
at Vernon and Main. He musters on up Main Street,
pleased with the symmetry of bricks, the correctness
of clapboards, the trim green of the common
with its bench. There he straightens his cap, bill back,
adjusts minutely the clipped cuffs of his pant legs, ready,
should a bicycle appear and need a rider.

But then at the center of the green he sees
a being from away in tights, filling herself
with fresh orange air, lifting a foot
to the other knee, folding her arms
across her chest, standing still as a sapling
in the center of its earth. She stares at nothing,
waiting for the sun to serve a private
and delicious light.

Dawn's deacon rises from his bench, resumes
his ritual path, inspector of fountain, curbs
and drains. It is for him to bring dawn to this
alien presence in the village morning, and he edges closer,
asking questions to himself, timid as an animal,
lest she be disturbed by his approach.

He tilts his head as if to better hear himself
or her, like a robin the stirring of a worm,
some subtle quaking in the ground to clarify
her sudden sprouting up amidst the damp grass,
and he fashions what he knows
for the familiar quiet.

Five miles on two legs I circle from my house
to center of town. You're in the center
on one leg—what's your name? Any fool knows
the job is walking clock and dawn
to lunch. Noon won't come to you
standing still, middle of the village, one leg
stuck in the ground.

They stand and watch their equal sun
climb the branches of a similar tree.
"Helps me center," her only words,
he listens again for the worm.

Every day I circle town—clouds or rain—
turn up to the center and listen. A thing moves
in its own dark. Can't find it and be it. I wait
till the sun gets free of its tree, then I take him
over the hill to my place. From there
he knows the way home
by himself.

Coming to Mr. Kirk

Before the crowd arrives I'll find shelter
among the thick trees and stand
very still.

The noise of them, the noise
bends the tall grass, though there is
no wind.

It's more than the advance of mice
in a meadow, unseen and many, or crows
opposing the morning's high opinion
of its clouds.

It's the rowdy tongues inside that drum
of unattended loves, chorus the day's alarms,
the prospect of sorrow, then chase their syllables
to dust in a chill sky that makes tears of them
for the rattle of rain.

The noise of them, the noise
offends a man standing in the simple shelter
of himself. I slip away to quiet
by a solitary man who fishes
the old way.

At the meadow's brook I know it's Mister Kirk
by the breadth of the britches high in the hitch of his galluses
and much above his boots.

Nor would I disturb the hat nesting in his gray hair
like a comfortable bird, for he stands very still, doesn't know
how the fishing is, and it won't likely improve, he says,
with a brass band close by.

There is but one of me, but the grass stirs, and he
with the wind's ear has heard it and enough, for he wears
a fill of years the crowd no longer counts, voices
the riffles have drowned out.

The water's tug is in his eye, and he cares to finish
with his fishing in a pool a ways downstream, smooth
and full of sky, where fish are leaping from their shadows
into the afternoon sun.

Re-cycling With Clayton

There is nothing in this world
you can't make into something
if you just collect the sundry species, types
and duplicates of things, particularly
extension cords and plugs.

Filled with that high purpose Clayton piloted
his personal ark, inviting nearly everything aboard
to house and porch and barn and nearby woods
to sail with him to new companionship and unimagined use.
It was clear his world preferred to turn around an axis
at an inclination unfamiliar to his neighbors
when he placed his rescued console television set
at a gentle list upon the driveway's center grass that lead
up to the barn, and there he watched it in the sun
and comfort of his re-cycled chaise. To him the tilt
was elementary as the three tall pines he rigged
with masts and yardarms of cast-off antennas
that filled his sails with Saturday operas lilting in the wind
to soothe a sailor on his restless sea.

On board already was the rabid porcupine
who lived beneath the kitchen floor, whom Clayton plied
with his best lettuce and who smiled benignly
through his froth, thinking himself divinely privy
to the marvels of a garden Clayton hid
from the eyes of thieves in holes and thickets
and those windows winking from beyond
the back stone wall.

But then he encountered footprints of those stealthy
neighbor boys from up the hill with predilections
for carrots flavored with cool dirt, and then of innocent deer
who knew no better than that Clayton's magic thumb
brought forth for them a paradise of green. But when
they mocked his moonlit twisting pie tins, Clayton
wired the garden up with seven speakers
thought gone silent at the dump and played
his favorite *La Bohème* to haunt the naughty boys
and fill the crescent moon with such ethereal voice,
the animals, stunned and tingling
in the singing of an almost empty moon,
forgot to eat.

But for the garden grown to utter loveliness,
for local beavers spared the trap, the gossipy birds
made happy in the flowering weeds left rampant
about the house where nothing merely annual
was allowed, the barn and porch fell down.

With loving inattention Clayton just smiled on
and bid them go, for his world was much and otherwise
afloat upon a sea of circumstance, sublime device
and all-belonging joy.

The Agony of the Fundamentalist Apple Grower

Ben believed, swore not
but by the Bible, whose chapter, verse
and taut apostles raise the numbered scaffolds
of a universe whose starry recompense
remits all doubt and trembling. It was a wonder
natural as his mother's famous apple pie or history
told in church to children who would one summer day
eagerly report upon the paths of the progenitors
they found in Maine's Natural History Museum.

Invited to the monthly evening congregation of their church,
two innocents reported on the way our distant forebears
lived in skin and fur of animals they ate, and using
tools of bone and stone some 20,000 years ago. "That
is a mistake," said Ben aloud, "too many zeroes!
Any more than three are only for money or counting
God's people. The Beginning began exactly
upon its written Word."

Summoned so to piety, he paused a precious moment
to abide in his and our beloved Paradise, the Bible's
narrative of apples, when suddenly a perilous uncertainty
fell due: the extra zero irrefutably recalled to him
the apple that so weakened Eve, and his
was now the burden to believe his mother's revelation
late in life that the divine temptations of her legendary
apple pie were not the fault of the apple
but the rum she put in the crust.

What instrument was it then that worked Evil
upon an innocent world? Where to curse, what
to praise? And certainly her pie had moved more men
than Ben to praise, high praise not lightly parceled out
upon this world sore hungry and afraid.

But he was a mother's loving son, a worshiper
of news revealed, a nimble monk most diligent
at splitting hairs in waiting on his Lord, and thus
of earthly pleasures he need not be redeemed
except from the luscious wonder of his mother's pie,
for it tasted better than a man should ever enjoy.

Thus Ben endured the torture of his own most urgent
questioning, for the story in the Bible is singular
and true, but the Tree of Knowledge now more difficult
for an apple orchard man whose very mother
altered the facts to spare the apple, laced the crust
to be more kind. Could she take back the bite
of such dire knowing, shorten a fall
into the truth?

Oh zero most excessive, apple too delicious
among others! The truth uncoiled its doubt,
and Adam smiled uncomfortably at Ben, his knowing
absolutely, as was his earthly lot, how rum in a crust
comes around the tongue and muddles the soul
past piety or faintest hope.

Nor was the sainted mother's mercy certain
as she said to him the recipe is less
than the goodness of a story, and you'll suffer best
the one that's your own.

Epilogue: The Absence of Strangers

I am of their multitude,
like you, and we keep them dear,
overheard or glimpsed or dreamed. Just out of reach
they take hands dancing us round and again
and ever after present. Absent yet,
they find our arms and legs, visit our eyes,
run in our blood. Some will want their say
and become words.

One is a dry old man, another a stone
grown large in the lift of frost. There is a woman
spry in the ripe terror of her loveliness, another
a shy bird, or the lady slipper stepping forth
from the shade of her inviolate strangeness
to find the warmth ephemeral and perilous
as the mind's hug or a kiss set free
without syntax or hour.

Uncommon incidents occur, we happen by
and don't blush, for history is done
with the baritone tale, a story's sultry step, the better
to disrupt us with a day's trivial events
and turn us wondering one to the other,
absent yet,

or else we might not notice, in the instant
a finger of air opens its leaves, the small nest
high in the limbs of a young tree, not pause
for a quiet about to speak, the footstep
in a rain's hush.

We are versed in the grammar of absence, the few words
scarring to beauty marks of a joy tenuous
and without end.

Richard Taylor

From growing up with Maine parents in rural New Hampshire, his education came from Dartmouth, the University of Kiel (Fulbright Fellowship) and Yale. He has been a teacher of German language and literature in colleges, Latin and English as well at private secondary schools. A member and captain of the 1964 Olympic Nordic Ski Team and for many years a staff coach with the National Team, he was variously a construction worker, ski touring center designer and operator, and for twenty years (through 2007) a teacher and running and cross-country ski coach at Gould Academy in Bethel, Maine. He lives with his wife Sally in Bethel.

www.ingramcontent.com/pod-product-compliance
Lightning Source LLC
Chambersburg PA
CBHW060533080526
44586CB00012B/717